P9-AQE-926

Crazy for
CAKE POPS

Crazy for CAKE POPS

50 *All–New Delicious and Adorable Creations*

MOLLY BAKES

Ulysses Press

Published in the United States by:
ULYSSES PRESS
P.O. Box 3440
Berkeley, CA 94703
www.ulyssespress.com

First published as *Cake Pops* in Great Britain in 2011 by Square Peg, a publisher in The Random House Group Ltd.

ISBN 978-1-61243-044-7
Library of Congress Control Number: 2011934777

Printed in the United States by Bang Printing

10 9 8 7 6 5 4 3 2 1

Photography: Noel Murphy
Interior design: Friederike Huber
Cover design: what!design @ whatweb.com
Prop Styling: Wei Tang
U.S. Editors: Elyce Berrigan-Dunlop, Lauren Harrison

This book is for the Mickeys and the Goodies

CONTENTS

INTRODUCTION

I am going to let you in on a little secret. I only learned to bake two years ago. That's right, I had never baked a single cake before then.

Here's how it came about: I had been obsessed with cupcakes for a while, so one Sunday afternoon a couple of years ago I asked my mother to teach me how to make them because she is a baking queen. That afternoon, some very simple vanilla cupcakes were baked and it all made perfect sense. From then on I was enchanted with baking beautiful, fluffy cakes. A month later I lost my job, the day before my 29th birthday. I might as well have cried but, secretly, I was not entirely unhappy about it. That night I went home and baked cupcakes for my birthday party. It took me until one o'clock in the morning just to bake and frost 30. But my friends loved them. Over the months that followed, the more I baked, the more I fell in love. That's when Molly Bakes was born.

Not long after setting up a stall for selling cupcakes in Brick Lane Market, in London's East End, I stumbled across something that would change my life for the second time: Cake Pops. I knew instantly that people would love these, and I was right. After a year of perfecting the Molly Bakes Cake Pop I was asked to write this book. And here it is—all the tricks for creating the perfect pop.

I hope my story and the recipes that follow show that you don't have to be a brilliant baker or even an experienced cake decorator to make these. All you need is a few simple ingredients, some lollipop sticks and a little imagination.

Enjoy popping! Molly Bakes

Cake pops are made by combining crumbled cake and frosting, then rolling the mixture into balls or other shapes and coating in candy or chocolate.

Once you have mastered the various steps for making cake pops, it opens up a whole new world of opportunities for sweet treats on a stick. All you need is a little patience and careful planning.

One of the many beauties of cake pops is they can be made in advance and the individual steps don't even need to be done on the same day. To make the perfect pop it's worth setting some time aside and preparing what you can ahead of time. Things such as rolling the cake pop mixture can be done up to three days before you decorate the pops. Just refrigerate and then bring it out when you feel like popping!

All the cake pop recipes in this book are based on making batches of 20 medium pops, or 10 large ones, depending on the nature of the design.

Once you get the hang of it, cake pops are very simple to make because every cake pop recipe follows the same basic steps:

- Bake a cake and allow to cool
- Make the frosting
- Thoroughly crumble the cake
- Combine the cake and frosting and refrigerate
- Roll mixture into balls and refrigerate
- Insert sticks into the balls
- Dip cake pops in candy
- Decorate
- Package and give as a gift or
- Eat!

This basic technique is used for all the styles in this book. Once you have mastered the simple cake ball, it's easy to create any shape you like, whether a square, rectangle, cone or oval.

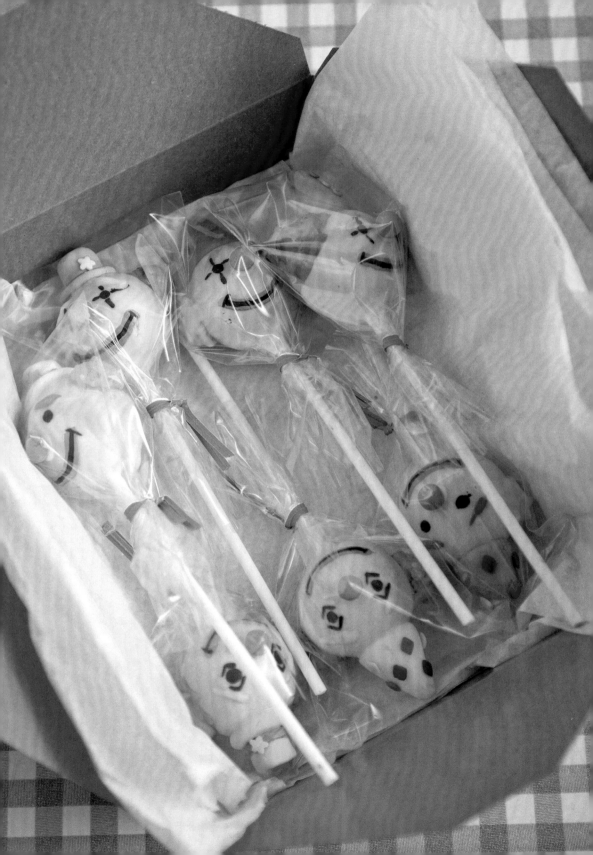

EQUIPMENT

Other than lollipop sticks and candy melts, you don't need any fancy equipment for making cake pops (and for the Chocolate Cake Balls on page 45 you don't even need those). If you have one, an electric mixer is an easy way of mixing the cake batter, but otherwise a hand whisk or even a wooden spoon is fine. You can find all the tools and ingredients you need in your local supermarket, in cake supply stores and online. A list of recommended suppliers is included on page 146. Later on, you might want to invest in more specialty tools such as different-shaped cutters, brushes and molds for creating elaborate shapes.

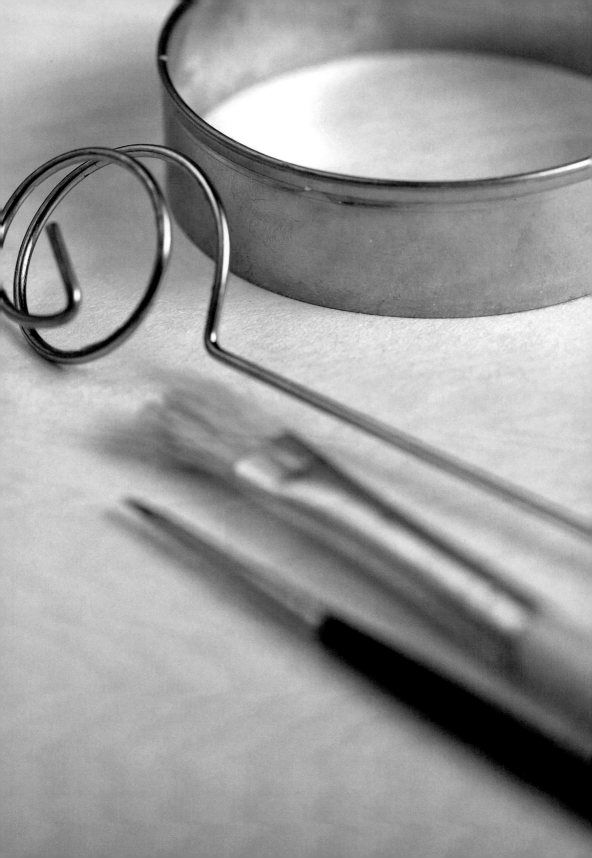

YOU WILL NEED

Cake baking tin
The shape of your cake tin doesn't matter—round or square, anything is fine since you'll be crumbling the cake anyway. A good size for these recipes is a 10-inch (25-centimeter) round tin or an 8-inch (20-centimeter) square one.

Large mixing bowl
For mixing the batter, then later for crumbling the cake sponge and mixing with frosting.

Microwave-safe mixing bowl(s)
Plastic bowls are best as ceramic or glass can get too hot and burn your hands. Make sure the bowl is microwave-safe for melting candy or chocolate.

Tray
For placing the rolled cake balls on when they are ready for dipping and during refrigeration. Any type of tray can be used.

Elevated metal wire rack
For cooling the cake sponge and for resting dipped cake balls on as they set.

Parchment paper
For lining trays and for placing under the wire rack to catch drips.

Plastic wrap
For wrapping the cake pop mixture during refrigeration.

Candy melts
Candy melts (also known as confectioner's chocolate or candy wafers) are a vegetable-oil-based product with similar properties to white chocolate. You can melt, mold, dip, drizzle and pipe candy melts. They come pre-colored in white, black, pink, red, blue, orange, yellow, green or brown and are widely available in all good cake supply stores. See page 136 for creating new colors too.

Vegetable oil
For adding to candy melts for a smooth consistency.

Plastic spatula

For scraping down the sides of the mixing bowl when mixing the cake batter and for stirring candy or chocolate.

Lollipop sticks

For inserting into the cake pops. You can get them from cake supply stores and some supermarkets.

Polystyrene block or floral foam

Poke holes into this so the cake pops can stand upright while they dry. Polystyrene is easiest to use and you can buy it from most craft stores. You can also use floral foam, but wrap it in plastic wrap so it doesn't get all over your hands and into the cake.

Toothpicks

Keep a supply of these on hand—they are useful when gluing decorations onto cake pops and for creating texture.

Useful Conversions

Measure	Equivalent	Metric
1 teaspoon	–	5 milliliters
1 tablespoon	3 teaspoons	14.8 milliliters
1 cup	16 tablespoons	236.8 milliliters
1 pint	2 cups	473.6 milliliters
1 quart	4 cups	947.2 milliliters
1 liter	4 cups + 3½ tablespoons	1000 milliliters
1 ounce (dry)	2 tablespoons	28.35 grams
1 pound	16 ounces	453.49 grams
2.21 pounds	35.3 ounces	1 kilogram
325°F/350°F/375°F	–	165°C/180°C/190°C

FLAVORS

The tried and tested recipes in this book are easy and you don't need to be an expert baker to make them. You're going to crumble the cake anyway so it doesn't matter whether it's even!

Feel free to mix the cake and frosting recipes as you wish, but I find that you get the best flavors when you match the cake and frosting, i.e., vanilla cake with vanilla frosting, peanut butter cake with peanut butter frosting, and so on. You'll get deeper flavors by doubling up.

If you can use good-quality ingredients when making these recipes, you'll really notice the difference in taste. I recommend butter instead of margarine, free-range eggs and vanilla extract instead of vanilla flavoring. You can also use organic flour, unrefined sugar and fairtrade organic cocoa powder (see page 146 for suppliers).

VANILLA CAKE

This light and fluffy vanilla cake makes a delicious base for a simple cake pop. Combine with classic vanilla cream cheese frosting for a wonderful buttery flavor.

Makes enough for approx. 20 medium cake balls

120 grams (½ cup) unsalted butter, softened, plus more for greasing
150 grams (⅔ cup) granulated sugar
1 teaspoon vanilla extract
2 eggs, at room temperature
180 grams (1⅓ cups) self-rising flour, sifted
4 tablespoons milk, at room temperature

Preheat the oven to 350°F (180°C). Lightly grease and flour a 10-inch (25-centimeter) round cake tin or an 8-inch (20-centimeter) square cake tin. Cream the butter and sugar until it turns pale and fluffy. Mix the vanilla extract into the creamed butter and sugar. Add the eggs, one at a time, mixing well between each addition. Add half the flour and then half the milk and mix until fully combined. Repeat with the remaining flour and milk.

Pour the mixture into the prepared tin and bake for 35–45 minutes, or until a toothpick inserted into the center of the cake comes out clean. Once baked, leave to cool in the tin for 20 minutes and then turn out onto a wire rack to finish cooling.

VANILLA CREAM CHEESE FROSTING

80 grams (⅓ cup) unsalted butter, softened
40 grams (2½ tablespoons) cream cheese, softened
200 grams (2 cups) powdered sugar, sifted
1 teaspoon vanilla extract

Cream the butter and cream cheese together. Gradually add the sugar, then continue to cream until light and fluffy. Finally, mix in the vanilla. Refrigerate for 30 minutes before using.

CHOCOLATE CAKE

This is a wonderfully rich chocolate cake, which creates my favorite baking aroma. Combine with the chocolate frosting for an unbelievably fudge-like texture.

Makes enough for approx. 20 medium cake balls

55 grams (8 tablespoons) cocoa powder
250 milliliters (1 cup) boiling water
120 grams (½ cup) unsalted butter, softened, plus more for greasing
200 grams (1 cup) granulated sugar
200 grams (1⅔ cups) self-rising flour, plus more for the tin
1 teaspoon baking powder
¼ teaspoon baking soda
¼ teaspoon salt
1 teaspoon vanilla extract
2 eggs, at room temperature

Put the cocoa into a heatproof bowl, pour in the boiling water and stir until combined. Set aside to cool. Preheat the oven to 375°F (190°C). Lightly grease and flour a 10-inch (25-centimeter) round cake tin. Sift together the flour, baking powder, baking soda and salt. Cream the butter and sugar until pale and fluffy. Mix in the vanilla. Add the eggs one at a time, mixing well. Pour in the dry ingredients and gently beat until combined. Fold in the cooled cocoa until the color of the mixture is even. Pour into the tin and bake for 45–60 minutes, or until a toothpick inserted into the center of the cake comes out clean. Once baked, leave to cool in the tin for 20 minutes. Turn out onto a wire rack to finish cooling.

CHOCOLATE FROSTING

120 grams (½ cup) unsalted butter, softened
200 grams (2 cups) powdered sugar, sifted
100 grams (1⅔ cups) chocolate, melted and cooled (see page 42)

Cream the butter. Gradually add the powdered sugar and then the chocolate. Continue to cream until light and fluffy. Refrigerate for 30 minutes before using.

RED VELVET CAKE

This traditional American cake flavor is perfect for Valentine's designs and is delicious combined with the vanilla cream cheese frosting on page 22.

Makes enough for approx. 20 medium cake balls

250 grams (2⅓ cups) self-rising flour, plus more for the tin
¼ teaspoon salt
1 tablespoon cocoa powder
4 tablespoon red food coloring
120 grams (½ cup) unsalted butter, softened, plus more for greasing
250 grams (1¼ cups) granulated sugar
2 eggs, at room temperature
240 milliliters (1 cup) buttermilk
1 teaspoon vanilla extract
1 teaspoon cider vinegar
1 teaspoon baking soda

Preheat the oven to 350°F (180°C). Lightly grease and flour a 10-inch (25-centimeter) round cake tin or an 8-inch (20-centimeter) square cake tin.

Sift together the flour and salt and set aside. In a cup or small bowl, mix the cocoa powder and red food coloring into a smooth paste, then set aside.

Cream the butter and sugar together until pale and fluffy. Add the eggs, one at a time, mixing well between each addition. Scrape down the sides of the bowl, then add the cocoa powder mixture.

In a measuring cup, whisk the buttermilk with the vanilla extract.

Now add a third of the flour mixture to the creamed butter and sugar, followed by half the buttermilk and mix until combined. Add another third of flour and the remaining buttermilk. Finally, add the remaining flour mixture and mix until just combined.

Combine the vinegar and baking soda in a small cup. Allow it to fizz and then quickly fold into the mixture. Pour into the prepared tin and bake for 30–45 minutes, or until a toothpick inserted into the center of the cake comes out clean.

Once baked, leave to cool in the tin for 20 minutes and then turn out onto a wire rack to finish cooling.

PEANUT BUTTER CAKE

Try this with peanut butter frosting or go for classic chocolate on page 25.

Makes enough for approx. 20 medium cake balls

180 grams (1⅓ cups) self-rising flour, plus more for the tin
1 teaspoon baking powder
80 grams (⅓ cup) unsalted butter, softened, plus more for greasing
50 grams (4½ tablespoons) smooth peanut butter
150 grams (⅔ cup) granulated sugar
2 eggs, at room temperature
125 milliliters (½ cup) milk

Preheat the oven to 350°F (180°C). Lightly grease and flour a 10-inch (25-centimeter) round cake tin or an 8-inch (20-centimeter) square cake tin.
    Sift together the flour and baking powder and set aside.
    Cream the butter and peanut butter until combined. Add the sugar and continue to cream until pale and fluffy. Add the eggs, one at a time, mixing well between each addition. Add half the flour, followed by half the milk and mix until combined. Repeat with the remaining flour and milk. Pour the mixture into the prepared tin and bake for 35–45 minutes, or until a toothpick inserted into the center of the cake comes out clean. Once baked, leave to cool in the tin for 20 minutes and then turn out onto a wire rack to finish cooling.

PEANUT BUTTER FROSTING

80 grams (⅓ cup) unsalted butter, softened
40 grams (3½ tablespoons) smooth peanut butter
200 grams (2 cups) powdered sugar
1 tablespoon milk

Cream the butter and peanut butter together. Gradually add the sugar, then continue to cream until light and fluffy. Finally, mix in the milk. Refrigerate for 30 minutes before using.

TOFFEE CAKE

Give your cake pops a traditional English twist with this mouthwatering toffee cake and creamy toffee frosting.

Makes enough for approx. 20 medium cake balls

200 grams (1⅔ cups) self-rising flour, plus more for the tin
1 teaspoon baking powder
150 grams (½ cup) unsalted butter, softened, plus more for greasing
150 grams (½ cup) light muscovado sugar
2 eggs, at room temperature
1 teaspoon vanilla extract
160 milliliters (⅔ cup) milk

Preheat the oven to 350°F (180°C). Lightly grease and flour a 10-inch (25-centimeter) round cake tin or an 8-inch (20-centimeter) square cake tin.

Sift the flour with the baking powder and set aside. Cream the butter and sugar together until pale and fluffy. Add the eggs, one at a time, mixing well between each addition. Mix in the vanilla extract. Add half the dry ingredients and then half the milk. Add the remaining dry ingredients, followed by the rest of the milk, and mix until combined. Pour the mixture into the prepared tin and bake for 35–40 minutes or until a toothpick inserted into the center comes out clean. Once baked, leave to cool in the tin for 20 minutes and then turn out onto a wire rack to finish cooling.

TOFFEE FROSTING

60 grams (¼ cup) unsalted butter, at room temperature
60 grams (3½ tablespoons) dulce de leche
200 grams (2 cups) powdered sugar

Cream the butter and dulce de leche together until well combined. Gradually add the powdered sugar and mix until smooth. Refrigerate for 30 minutes before using.

LEMON CAKE

My much-loved lemon cake recipe is a favorite in the spring. Combine it with zesty lemon frosting and try it with the Easter Bunnies.

Makes enough for approx. 20 medium cake balls

200 grams (1⅔ cups) self-rising flour, plus more for the tin
1 teaspoon baking powder
¼ teaspoon baking soda
½ teaspoon salt
120 grams (½ cup) unsalted butter, softened, plus more for greasing
200 grams (1 cup) granulated sugar
Zest of 1 lemon
2 eggs, at room temperature
125 milliliters (½ cup) full-fat yogurt

Preheat the oven to 350°F (180°C). Lightly grease and flour a 10-inch (25-centimeter) round cake tin or an 8-inch (20-centimeter) square cake tin.
　Sift together the flour, baking powder, baking soda and salt. Set aside.
　Cream the butter and sugar until pale and fluffy. Mix in the lemon zest, then add the eggs, one at a time, mixing well between each addition. Now add the dry ingredients in 1 batch and mix until just combined. Fold in the yogurt. Pour the mixture into the prepared tin and bake for 35–45 minutes, or until a toothpick inserted into the center of the cake comes out clean. Once baked, leave to cool in the tin for 20 minutes and then turn out onto a wire rack to finish cooling.

LEMON FROSTING

120 grams (½ cup) unsalted butter, softened   Zest of 1 lemon
200 grams (2 cups) powdered sugar   1 tablespoon milk

Cream the butter until very soft. Gradually add the sugar and then continue to cream the mixture until it is light and fluffy. Mix in the zest and finally the milk. Refrigerate for 30 minutes before using.

METHOD

Once you have baked your cake and made your frosting, follow these steps to make your cake pop mixture, to shape the cake balls and to coat them. A great trick is that you don't have to do all of this on the same day. The mixture stores well, so you can prepare it in advance and make your cake pop designs another day.

COMBINE THE CAKE WITH THE FROSTING

Once you have the baked cake and frosting ready you can proceed to the next step of the cake pop process.

Crumble your cake thoroughly in a large mixing bowl. I normally do this by hand as it gives a finer crumb, but you can also use your food processor. You may want to remove the crusts of the cake with a sharp kitchen knife first to avoid any lumps.

Once you have crumbled the cake as finely as possible, take your frosting, a heaping tablespoon at a time, and begin mixing it in with the crumbs. You may not require all of the frosting, depending on how moist your cake is, so just use a little at a time. Keep mixing until you have a fudge-like texture. To see if it's ready, squeeze a little of the mixture in your palm—it shouldn't crumble and it should be pliable. If you add too much frosting your mixture will be soggy, sticky and heavy and the cake pops will just fall off the stick when you try to dip them.

Wrap the mixture in plastic wrap and chill for at least 1 hour. When the mixture is firm but not too hard, it's ready to work with.

ROLL THE CAKE BALLS

Break off a small piece of the mixture, about the size of a ping-pong ball, and roll into a ball with your palms. It doesn't have to be perfect.

Place each ball on a tray lined with parchment paper. Refrigerate for 15–20 minutes, or until they are firm.

You can either go ahead and just dip them as they are to make simple cake balls, or shape them into a more adventurous design. In the Techniques chapter on page 132 I explain how to roll other shapes.

PREPARE THE CANDY MELTS

When using candy melts, it's important to make sure that all of your equipment, such as bowls and spatulas, is completely dry.

To melt the candy, you will need:

1 (14-ounce) bag candy melts
Vegetable oil
Microwave-safe bowl
Plastic spatula

Place the candy melts in a microwave-safe bowl and heat in the microwave on medium power for 1 minute. Take out the candy melts and stir thoroughly. They may have just started to melt. Place back in the microwave and melt for another 30 seconds. Stir again, making sure you scrape the bottom and sides of the bowl. Return to the microwave for another 30 seconds, then give a final stir.

Melted candy doesn't normally achieve the same silky, runny consistency of melted chocolate. To make it easier to work with, you can add 1–2 tablespoons of vegetable oil per 14-ounce bag of candy melts. Work enough oil into the candy with your spatula to create a silky consistency.

Candy will stay melted for about 20–30 minutes. If you stir your candy at regular intervals while working, it should keep from hardening. See page 137 for tips such as reheating candy melts.

INSERT LOLLIPOP STICKS

Take a lollipop stick and dip one end about ¾ inch deep into the melted candy. Immediately insert the stick into the top center of each cake ball, about halfway through. Don't insert it too deep or too shallow. Place on a tray lined with parchment paper to set. It should take 1–2 minutes for the candy to set.

DIP THE CAKE POPS

Before you start it's best to pierce the holes into the polystyrene block that will hold the cake pops. This will save time and prevent accidents. Simply use a lollipop stick to pierce holes about 2 inches apart.

To dip cake pops in the melted candy make sure the bowl is deep and quite full with candy so you don't need to tilt it. Hold an undipped cake pop by the stick and dip fully into the candy. When dipping, be sure to cover right to the top of the stick to secure the pop in place.

Gently tap the cake pop over the bowl to remove any excess candy. Place securely in the polystyrene block and allow to dry. Candy should take only 1–2 minutes to set.

DECORATE THE CAKE POPS

You can decorate with sprinkles or sugar decorations before the candy has set or leave the cake pops to dry completely if you're making one of the other more elaborate designs in the book.

To decorate with sprinkles, simply take a teaspoonful of sprinkles and scatter them over the cake pop with a soft shake of your wrist. To decorate with sugar decorations, just press the decoration in the position of your choice, then place the pop in the polystyrene block to set.

See Techniques on page 132 for other tips on making fondant decorations and on using cocoa butter for painting the cake pops. There you'll also find details of other equipment and ingredients you might need when tackling the more adventurous cake pop designs in this book.

DESIGNS

Start off with simple round cake pops and from there the pop world is your oyster. Why not try Sweethearts for Valentine's Day, Teddy Bears for a baby shower, Ice Cream Cone Pops for a sunny day or Tricolor Pops just because.

SIMPLE POPS

Chocolate is a simple and easy-to-find alternative to candy melts for making cake pops. Try them with white, milk or dark to intensify the flavors. Decorate with nuts, candied orange or crystallized rose petals, or drizzle with chocolate for a sophisticated gourmet pop!

Try these as cake pops or upside-down pops.

Makes 20 pops

Ingredients
20 medium cake balls, chilled
400 grams (1⅔ cups) good-quality chocolate (white, milk or dark)
Decorations of your choice

Break up the chocolate into small pieces and place in a microwave-safe bowl. Heat in the microwave for 1 minute on the medium setting. Stir and repeat until chocolate has melted.

   Dip the end of each lollipop stick ¾ inch deep into the chocolate and insert about halfway into the center of each cake ball. Allow to set. Dip each cake pop into the melted chocolate, making sure the entire cake is coated, then remove and gently shake off any excess into the bowl. Decorate with sprinkles, nuts or confections of your choice. You can either insert into a polystyrene block or place face down onto parchment paper to make upside-down pops. They will take 5 minutes to dry.

CAKE BALLS

What's brilliant about Cake Balls is that they stand deliciously on their own—no need to make them into pops. All you need is chocolate to coat them. If you've got prepared cake balls in your fridge but don't have time to visit your local cake supply shop to find lollipop sticks, here's your solution—simple but oh so good.

Makes 20 cake balls

Ingredients
20 medium cake balls, chilled
400 grams (1⅔ cups) good-quality chocolate (white, milk or dark)
Decorations of your choice

Break up the chocolate into small pieces and place in a microwave-safe bowl. Heat for 1 minute on the medium setting. Stir and repeat until chocolate has melted.
   Place a sheet of parchment paper under a wire rack. Dip the cake balls into the melted chocolate using a toothpick. Make sure the entire cake ball gets coated in chocolate. Leaving the toothpicks in the balls, gently shake off any excess chocolate into the bowl. Decorate with sprinkles, nuts or confections of choice. Run the toothpicks through the wire rack and leave to set for at least 5 minutes. Once the chocolate has set, remove the toothpicks.

SWEETHEART POPS

Inspired by the candies of the same name, these cake pops can be personalized for any occasion.

Makes 20 pops

Ingredients
20 medium cake balls, chilled
1 (14-ounce) bag candy melts in base color of your choice
¼ (14-ounce) bag red candy melts

Equipment
2-inch round pastry cutter
Piping bag

For each cake ball, flatten and shape it into a ¾-inch-thick circle by pushing it into the pastry cutter. Remove and smooth the edges with moistened fingers. Place in the fridge for 10 minutes to harden.

Melt the candy melts in the base color. Dip each lollipop stick ¾ inch deep into the melted candy and insert a stick through the center of each cake pop. Leave for 1–2 minutes until the candy has set.

Now dip each cake pop fully into the melted candy, making sure they get coated evenly. Remember to gently shake off any excess candy into the bowl, then place in a polystyrene block to dry.

Melt the red candy melts, then quickly pour into the piping bag so the candy doesn't set. Cut a small piece off the tip of the bag. Place a cake pop on a flat surface. Pipe the outline of a heart shape on the pop and then pipe Sweethearts messages. Repeat with the remaining pops.

TRICOLOR POPS

Simple but very effective. Try this with contrasting colors of candy or varying shades of one color.

Makes 20 pops

Ingredients
20 medium cake balls, chilled
1 (14-ounce) bag candy melts in base color of your choice
½ (14-ounce) bag candy melts in a second color
½ (14-ounce) bag candy melts in a third color

Melt the base color of candy. Dip the end of each lollipop stick ¾ inch deep into the candy and insert a stick about halfway into the center of each cake ball. Leave to set.

Now dip each cake ball into the base color of candy, remembering to gently tap the excess into the bowl. Insert into a polystyrene block to dry. Drying time should be between 1 and 2 minutes.

Melt the second and third colors of candy separately. Now dip the top two-thirds of each cake pop into a contrasting or lighter/darker color of candy. Make sure you dip straight down, to create even lines. Gently tap the excess into the bowl and insert into the polystyrene block to dry.

Finally, dip the top third of each cake pop into the third color of candy. Gently tap off the excess and insert into the polystyrene block to dry.

If you want to take it further, why not try creating rainbows or flags with the different colors of candy.

MARBLE POPS

Marbling is another simple technique that will brighten up a basic round cake pop. You can start off with two colors and add as many as you like for total marble madness.

Makes 20 pops

Ingredients
20 medium cake balls, chilled
1 (14-ounce) bag candy melts in base color of your choice
¼ (14-ounce) bag candy melts in secondary color of your choice

Melt the base color of candy. Dip the end of each lollipop stick ¾ inch deep into the melted candy and insert a stick about halfway into the center of each cake ball. Leave to set.

Melt the secondary color of candy and, using a tablespoon, add a little of the secondary color to the bowl containing the base color. Then use a toothpick to create swirls in the candy, taking care not to overmix the colors.

Slowly dip each cake ball fully into the melted candy and, as you dip, twirl it in the candy so that the colors swirl. This will create a gorgeous marble effect. Gently tap the excess candy into the bowl and insert the pop into a polystyrene block to dry.

Once you have mastered one extra color, you can try experimenting with two secondary colors.

CLOUD POPS

Clouds are light and fluffy—just like cake—so one day I thought why not turn cake into clouds? Eureka!

Makes 10 pops

Ingredients
10 medium cake balls, chilled
1 (14-ounce) bag white candy melts

Break up each cake ball and roll into 17 small, different-sized balls. Keep these small balls together in sets.

Melt the white candy. For each cloud, stick 7 balls together in a flat, horizontal cluster, using the candy as glue. Then make a separate cluster of 5 balls and stick it on the top of the first 7. Make a third cluster of 3 balls and glue it on top of the 5-ball cluster. Finally, stick the last 2 remaining balls on the topmost layer, again using the candy as glue. Leave on a tray lined with parchment paper to set.

Dip the end of each lollipop stick 1 inch deep into the candy and, taking extra care, insert a stick into each cloud. Leave to set.

Now dip each pop fully into the candy and gently tap off any excess. Insert into a polystyrene block to dry.

LIGHTNING POPS

The weather forecasters might often get it wrong but these bolts are simple to make and you can be sure they'll always taste great.

Makes 20 pops

Ingredients
20 medium cake balls, chilled
1 (14-ounce) bag yellow candy melts

Split each cake ball in half and shape each half into a triangular wedge about ¾ inch thick. Keep the wedges in pairs. For each pair, square off the pointed edge of one of the wedges with a knife and elongate the pointed edge of the second wedge.

Melt the yellow candy. Place a pair of wedges side by side, with the squared-off wedge on the left and the longer wedge about two-thirds of the way down on the right so you have something resembling a lightning bolt. Keep them in this position as you stick them together, using a dab of candy on a toothpick to secure them. Repeat for each pair of wedges.

One by one, dip the end of each lollipop stick ¾ inch deep into the candy, then take hold of a lightning bolt diagonally and insert the stick through the center. Leave to set.

Dip each pop fully into the candy and shake off the excess. Insert into a polystyrene block to dry.

PRESENTS

Everyone loves presents. Make these extra-pretty with bows and polka dots.

Makes 20 presents

Ingredients
20 medium cake balls, chilled
¼ (14-ounce) bag each pink, yellow,
   blue and green candy melts
50 grams (¼ cup) white fondant,
   kneaded
Edible glue
1 bottle white cocoa butter

Equipment
Rolling pin
2 paintbrushes (1 thin, 1 medium)
Artist's palette

Make bows in advance: Roll out three-quarters of the fondant to ¹/₁₆ inch thick. Using a kitchen or small palette knife, cut it into 20 strips about 1½ inches long and ½ inch wide. Fold the ends of each strip so they meet in the middle to form a bow, and apply some edible glue with a paintbrush to stick them in place. Now roll out the remaining fondant to ¹/₁₆ inch thick and cut into 20 strips, each about ¾ inch long and ¼ inch wide. Wrap a strip around the center of each bow and glue into place. Place on a tray lined with parchment paper and leave to set overnight.

Using your hands, shape half the cake balls into squares and the other half into rectangles. Leave to chill for 10 minutes.

Place a sheet of parchment paper under a wire rack. Melt the different colors of candy separately. Insert a toothpick into each square. Working with 5 squares per color, dip each fully into the candy and shake off the excess. Place a bow on top of each one as you go and run the toothpicks through the wire rack. Leave to set.

Melt the cocoa butter and pour 1 teaspoonful into the palette. Paint a vertical white ribbon down the center of each side of the cake.

One by one, take hold of each square by its toothpick and paint dots, swirls, stars and other patterns on it. Remove the sticks, then put them on a tray lined with parchment paper and place in the fridge until the cocoa butter has set.

BAUBLE POPS

Baubles are beautiful party decorations for any time of year. Make them sparkle with a little edible luster spray.

Makes 20 pops

Ingredients
20 medium cake balls, chilled
¼ (14-ounce) bag each green, blue, pink and yellow candy melts
40 grams (2½ tablespoons) white fondant, kneaded
1 can edible silver luster spray

Equipment
4 disposable piping bags

Make tops of baubles in advance: Split the fondant into 20 pieces and roll into balls with your hands. Flatten the balls slightly and make a hole through the middle of each one using the end of a lollipop stick. Leave to harden for a few hours. Once hardened, spray with the silver luster spray. Leave to set overnight.

Melt each color of candy separately. Working with 5 cake balls per color, dip the end of each lollipop stick ¾ inch deep into the candy and insert a stick into each cake ball. Leave to set.

Dip each cake ball fully into the candy, shake off any excess and, while the candy is still wet, slide a bauble top down over the stick. Make sure the bauble top sticks firmly to the candy on the ball. Place on a sheet of parchment paper with the stick facing up.

Working with 1 color of candy at a time, pour each color into a separate piping bag. Cut a small piece off the tip of each bag and pipe designs onto the cake pops.

Once the candy has set, spray the cake pops lightly with the silver luster spray.

FAT BIRD POPS

Tweet tweet! These birds were loosely inspired by a certain social networking website.

Makes 20 pops

Ingredients
20 medium cake balls, chilled
1 ounce bag each yellow and orange candy melts
Small edible heart sprinkles, for the beaks
1 bottle white cocoa butter
1 tube brown or black edible dusting powder

Equipment
Thin paintbrush
Artist's palette

For each cake ball, break off a 1-tablespoon piece and split it in half. Shape each half into an elongated teardrop and then curve into a wing shape. Use the rest of the cake ball for the bird's body and elongate the back to form the tail.

Melt the 2 colors of candy separately. Dab a little candy on each wing with a toothpick and secure in place on the bird's body, pointed side up. Leave to set.

Working with 10 pops per color, dip the end of each lollipop stick ¾ inch deep into the candy and insert a stick into each cake pop. Leave to set.

Now dip each pop fully into its respective candy color. Insert into a polystyrene block to dry.

Using 2 heart sprinkles per cake pop, dip the curved end of each heart into the candy. Attach to the front of each pop to make the beaks.

Melt the cocoa butter and tint 1 teaspoonful with the dusting powder. Paint dots for the eyes. If you like, you can use other colors to paint patterns on the wings.

TROPICAL FISH POPS

What could be more colorful than these tropical fish? Try painting stripes, dots and even scales. Spray with edible luster for an iridescent look.

Makes 20 pops

Ingredients
20 medium cake balls, chilled
¼ (14-ounce) bag each pink, green, yellow and orange candy melts
1 bottle white cocoa butter
1 tube each black, purple and blue edible dusting powder
1 can edible pearl luster spray (optional)

Equipment
2 paintbrushes (1 thin, 1 medium)
Artist's palette

Break off a 1-tablespoon piece from each cake ball and set aside. Form the larger ball into a large heart shape for the body. Shape the pointed end of the heart into a bulb for the mouth. Pinch and elongate the top curved edge to make the fin. Make sure the bottom of the fish is wide enough to push a stick into. Now take the reserved small balls and shape each one into a "V," then curve each side outwards to form the tail.

Melt the 4 colors of candy separately. Working with 5 cake pops per color, use a little candy to secure the tails to the back of the pops. Leave to set.

Dip the end of each lollipop stick ¾ inch deep into the candy and insert a stick halfway through the bottom of each fish. Leave to set. Then dip each pop fully into the candy and shake off the excess. Insert into a polystyrene block to dry.

Melt the cocoa butter. In the palette, tint 1 teaspoonful each with the 3 dusting powders and leave 1 teaspoonful white. Use the white color to paint large dots for the fish eyes. Leave to dry and then paint a smaller dot inside the eye with the black color. Use the purple and blue colors to paint tropical accents, stripes and dots on the pops. Insert into the polystyrene block and place in the fridge until the cocoa butter has set.

When set, spray each pop with pearl luster if you wish, then place back in the polystyrene block to dry.

LIP POPS

Pucker up! Lip pops provide a lot of fun. Make them as a set with the moustaches—they are a great gift for a newlywed couple.

Makes 20 pops

Ingredients
20 medium cake balls, chilled
½ (14-ounce) bag each red and pink candy melts

For each pair of lips, mold each cake ball into the shape of an eye. Using a lollipop stick, make a slight indentation in the topmost curve of the "eye." Next, make an indentation running horizontally along the front. Finally, pinch the corners of the "eye" and shape each corner upwards so you end up with something resembling a pair of lips.

   Melt the 2 colors of candy separately. Working with 10 pops per color, dip the end of each lollipop stick ¾ inch deep into the candy and insert a stick into each pair of lips. Leave to set. Dip each pop fully into its respective color of candy and gently shake off any excess. Insert into a polystyrene block to dry.

MOUSTACHE POPS

A pop that's fit for a true gent. Who said cake pops were just for the ladies?

Makes 20 pops

Ingredients
20 medium cake balls, chilled
1 (14-ounce) bag black candy melts

Roll each cake ball into a log shape with your hands. Use a lollipop stick to make an indentation in the top center and bottom center of each "log." Squeeze and pinch the center of the "log" to shape the middle of the moustache. Now squeeze and pinch the ends, curling each one upwards to create a handlebar moustache shape.

   Melt the candy. Dip the end of each lollipop stick ¾ inch into the candy and insert a stick into the center of each moustache. Leave to set. Dip each pop into the candy, dipping from left to right to get an even coating. Insert into a polystyrene block to dry.

VINTAGE BUTTON POPS

I love all things vintage and these buttons remind me of Parisian flea markets. These cake pops have become the signature look of Molly Bakes. You can use silicone molds to make the buttons or get creative and make your own shapes.

Makes 20 pops

Ingredients
20 medium cake balls, chilled
¼ (14-ounce) bag each pink, yellow, lavender and green candy melts
50 grams (¼ cup) fondant
Food coloring paste
Edible sprinkles of your choice

Equipment
1 or 2 vintage button molds

Prepare the fondant buttons in advance: take the fondant, color it with the food coloring paste and knead it. Push a piece into each hole in the mold(s), cutting off any excess with a small knife. Leave to dry on parchment paper. Cover with plastic wrap and store in a cool, dry place until ready to use.

When ready to make the pops, melt each color of candy melts separately. Dip 5 lollipop sticks ¾ inch deep into the pink candy and insert halfway into the center of 5 cake balls. Repeat, using 5 sticks per candy color.

One by one, dip the cake pops fully into the different colors of candy, so you end up with 5 pink, 5 yellow, 5 lavender and 5 green pops, and decorate with the buttons. Sprinkle with colored confetti sugar or sprinkles.

Insert the pops into a polystyrene block to dry.

HANDBAG POPS

Treat yourself and your fashionista friends to miniature edible versions of your favorite "it" bag.

Makes 20 pops

Ingredients
20 medium cake balls, chilled
¼ (14-ounce) bag each white, pink and lavender candy melts
¼ (14-ounce) bag black or brown candy melts
80 grams (⅓ cup) black or brown fondant, kneaded

Equipment
Disposable piping bag

Make handles in advance: roll the fondant into a log shape with your hands. With a small knife, cut into 20 strips, making some 1½ inches long and others ¾ inch long, then form each piece into a "U" shape. Leave on parchment paper to dry overnight.

Shape each cake ball into a rectangle with slanted sides. Try making some rectangles longer or wider than others for variety.

Melt each color of candy melts separately. Working with 5 pops per color, dip the end of each lollipop stick ¾ inch into the candy and insert a stick through the bottom of each pop. Leave to set. Dip each pop fully into its respective color of candy and shake off any excess. Insert into a polystyrene block to dry.

Quickly pour the remaining black or brown candy into the piping bag. Cut a small piece off the tip and pipe details such as seams, clasps and logos on the bags. Use the candy in the piping bag to attach the handles to each bag. Place the pops back in the polystyrene block to set.

ICE CREAM CONE POPS

Perfect for a picnic on a sunny day. Add a fun and realistic touch with drips of candy and colorful sprinkles.

Makes 10 pops

Ingredients
10 small cake balls
10 medium cake balls
½ (14-ounce) bag each light brown and white candy melts
½ (14-ounce) bag pink, yellow and lavender candy melts
Sprinkles

Roll each medium cake ball between your palms into a cone shape. Repeat with the rest of the medium balls.

Push one side of each small cake ball onto a flat surface to flatten it slightly. Repeat with the rest of the small balls.

To assemble the ice cream pops: melt and mix together all of the light brown candy and three-quarters of the white candy to make a caramel color. Dip the end of each lollipop stick ¾ inch into the candy. Insert halfway into the thinner end of the cone. Now dip the surface of the top end of the cone into the candy and stick the flat side of a small cake ball onto it. Repeat with each pop and once the candy has set, dip the entire thing into the bowl. Insert into a polystyrene block to dry.

Now melt separately the pink, yellow and lavender candy and dip the top third of the cake pop, just to where the small ball meets the cone, into your chosen color. If you're feeling adventurous, holding the pop vertically, tap the bottom of the stick onto your kitchen surface. This will create fantastically authentic-looking ice cream drips.

Melt the rest of the white candy melts with an extra drop of vegetable oil. Using a teaspoon, drizzle over the top of the ice cream pop. Give it a little shake to create drips. Top with sprinkles.

To finish, take a toothpick and softly score diagonal lines across the cone to give a diamond pattern.

DONUT POPS

Double the sweetness, and who can say no to a donut? Combine the two for a totally poptastic treat.

Makes 20 pops

Ingredients
20 medium cake balls, chilled
1 (14-ounce) bag light brown candy melts
½ (14-ounce) bag white candy melts
Edible sprinkles, to decorate

Equipment
Medium ball tool

Take the cake balls and flatten them to form a donut shape. Next take the ball tool and gently push it into the center of the donut to make a dent. Make sure you make enough of a dent for it to show through when the pop has been dipped in the candy. Chill for 10 minutes.

Melt and mix together the brown candy melts and three-quarters of the white candy melts to create a caramel color.

Dip the end of each lollipop stick ¾ inch deep into the melted candy and insert a stick through the side of each donut about halfway in. Leave to set. Dip the donut pops in the candy and tap off the excess into the bowl. Place in a polystyrene block to dry.

In a separate bowl, melt the rest of the white candy. It's important that this is runnier than usual so add an extra drop of vegetable oil. Now take the teaspoon and drizzle the candy around the dent of the donuts. Shake on the sprinkles as you go. Place the pops back in the polystyrene block to dry.

TEA PARTY POPS

Afternoon tea has never been more popular. What could be a more fitting companion than your very own tea party set of cake pops?

Makes 10 teapots and 10 cups and saucers

Ingredients
20 medium cake balls, chilled
1 (14-ounce) bag white candy melts
100 grams (½ cup) fondant, kneaded and tinted pink
Edible glue
1 bottle white cocoa butter
1 tube edible dusting powder

Equipment
Rolling pin
1½-inch round fondant cutter
2 paintbrushes (1 thin, 1 medium)
Artist's palette

Make in advance
Saucers: roll out half the fondant to ⅛-inch thick and cut out 20 circles with the fondant cutter. Using the end of a lollipop stick, poke holes the same size as the sticks into the middle of the circles.
Handles: roll out a long, thin log shape with half the remaining fondant. Cut out 10 1½-inch-long pieces for the teapot handles and 10 1¼-inch-long pieces for the teacup handles. Form each handle into a "C" shape.
Domed lids and knobs: using the remaining fondant, roll 10 1-inch-diameter balls of fondant with your hands. Cut off the top third and bottom third of each ball— this will give you 20 domes for the lids. Roll 20 ³/₁₆-inch-diameter balls for the knobs, using your hands, and glue to the top center of each dome, dabbing on the edible glue with the thin paintbrush.

For the teapots

Take 10 of the chilled cake balls and separate a small (1-teaspoon) piece of mixture from each ball. Re-roll the larger balls and squash the bottom of each ball down flat.

For the teapot spouts, take the 10 (1-teaspoon) pieces of cake pop mixture and roll each piece into a log shape with your thumb and forefinger. Shape it so that one end of the log is thinner than the other. Set aside in the fridge.

For the teacups

Take the remaining 10 chilled cake balls and place on a flat surface, pushing the bottom of each ball down on the surface. You want the top of the cups to be completely flat, so push down and smooth the sides down until you get a half-ball shape. Set aside in the fridge.

Melt the white candy melts. Remove the teacup and teapot shapes from the fridge. Using a toothpick, dab a little candy on the thicker end of the spouts and attach them to the teapots. Make sure they are facing the right way up.

Dip the end of each lollipop stick ¾ inch deep into the candy. Insert a stick into the flatter end of each teapot and into the round end of each teacup.

Dip each teapot fully into the candy. Be extra gentle so that the spout doesn't fall off. Attach the lids to the teapots before the candy sets.

Next, dip each teacup into the candy and attach the saucers to the bottom of the teacups by sliding them up the sticks.

Insert each cake pop into a polystyrene block to dry—1–2 minutes per pop.

Once the cake pops have dried, attach the handles by using a small dab of candy on a toothpick to secure them.

Melt the cocoa butter and tint 1 teaspoonful with the dusting powder. Use the thicker paintbrush to paint beautiful vintage-style patterns on the teapots with the cocoa butter. Keep it simple—dots, swirls and stripes all look really cute.

SLICE OF CAKE POPS

It might be stating the obvious, but I love cake, so it's only right that a slice gets featured in this book! Choose any flavor of cake you like for these pops—vanilla, chocolate, red velvet, toffee, lemon or even peanut butter.

Makes 20 pops

Ingredients
20 medium cake balls, chilled
½ (14-ounce) bag each white and brown candy melts
20 red Smarties
Multi-colored edible sprinkles
2 ounces pink or red candy melts

Equipment
2 disposable piping bags

Shape each cake ball into a wedge with the shorter side of the wedge slightly rounded.

Melt the white and brown candy separately. Dip 10 lollipop sticks ¾ inch deep into the brown candy and the other 10 sticks ¾ inch deep into the white candy and insert a stick into the center of each wedge. Leave to set. Now dip each pop fully into the candy, dipping 10 pops into the brown and 10 into the white, and shake off the excess. Insert into a polystyrene block to dry.

Dip the top ⅜ inch of each white cake pop into the brown candy, then dip the top ⅜ inch of the rounded edge into the candy. Place a Smartie on top of each pop and decorate with sprinkles as you go. Do the same with the brown cake pops but dip them into the white candy. Place back in the polystyrene block to dry.

Melt the pink or red candy. Pour into the piping bag and cut a small piece off the tip. Pipe a pink or red horizontal line across the sides of each cake pop. Do the same with the remaining white candy. Place back in the polystyrene block to set.

SUSHI

These sushi-inspired cake balls look so realistic you could serve them as canapés at your next party and astonish all your guests.

Makes 20 pieces of sushi

Ingredients
20 medium cake balls, chilled
1 (14-ounce) bag white candy melts
¼ (14-ounce) bag each orange and red candy melts
White sugar strands or sprinkles
50 grams (¼ cup) black fondant, kneaded

Equipment
Rolling pin
Small palette knife

Split each cake ball in half. Keeping them in pairs, shape each half into a rectangular block—they can be irregular sizes.

Melt the white candy. Stick each pair of blocks together, using the candy as glue, and insert a toothpick into each sushi piece. Leave to set. Place a sheet of parchment paper under a wire rack. Holding it by the toothpick, dip each piece fully into the white candy and shake off the excess. Run the toothpick through the wire rack and leave to set.

Melt the orange and red candy separately. Dip the top half of 10 sushi pieces into the red candy and the other 10 into the orange candy. While the orange candy is still wet, use a toothpick to draw chevrons on it with the white candy. Give it a gentle shake to smooth it out. Return to the wire rack to dry.

Dab the remaining white candy around the bottom of each piece, sprinkling the white sugar strands as you go. Remove the toothpicks and leave to set.

Roll out the black fondant and cut out 20 strips about ⅝ inch wide and 4 inches long. Working quickly before the fondant dries, wrap them around the side of each piece. Place on a tray lined with parchment paper to set.

FLOWERPOT POPS

Ideal for Mother's Day, these beautiful flowerpots are a more inspired choice than the traditional bouquet. You can make the roses yourself or buy ready-made ones.

Makes 20 pops

Ingredients
20 medium cake balls
½ (14-ounce) bag each orange
   and red candy melts
2 ounces green candy melts
25 grams (1½ tablespoons) each of
   white and pink (or yellow and
   lavender) fondant, kneaded

Equipment
Rolling pin
Small palette knife
Disposable piping bag

Make roses in advance: roll out the 2 colors of fondant to $\frac{1}{16}$ inch thick. With a palette knife, cut out 40 strips of each color, about ¾ inch wide and 4 inches long. Using your fingers, roll each strip into simple rose shapes. You will need 4 roses per cake pop.

For each cake ball, break off a 2-tablespoon piece and set aside. Roll the rest of the ball into a log shape. Make one end of the "log" thinner than the other end to form the bottom of the flowerpot.

Take the small piece of cake ball, reroll it and flatten into a ¼-inch-thick circle so that it is slightly bigger than the top of the flowerpot.

Melt the orange and red candy melts together. Dip the top of each flowerpot into the candy and stick the flat circles on top. Leave to set. Dip the end of each lollipop stick ¾ inch deep into the candy and insert a stick into the bottom of each pop. Leave to set. Then dip each pop fully into the candy and insert into a polystyrene block to dry.

Using a dab of candy on a toothpick as glue, arrange the roses on top of the flowerpot and secure in place.

Melt the green candy. Quickly pour into the piping bag, cut a small piece off the tip and pipe leaves around the roses. Place the pops back in the polystyrene block to set.

SHEEP

Create your own pop farm with these sheep. They require a little more patience than the other designs, so set aside some extra time.

Makes 20 sheep

Ingredients
20 medium cake balls, chilled
1 (14-ounce) bag white candy melts
½ (14-ounce) bag black candy melts
20 small edible heart sprinkles
40 M&M's
1 bottle cocoa butter
1 tube each pink and black edible
 dusting powder

Equipment
Thin paintbrush
Artist's palette

Break a 2½-teaspoon piece from each cake ball and roll it for the head. Melt the white candy. Insert a toothpick into each larger cake ball, then dip fully into the candy and shake off any excess. Run the toothpicks through a wire rack placed over a sheet of parchment paper and leave to set.

Dip each larger cake ball once more into the candy, using a toothpick to texturize the candy before it sets. Build up layers of curls.

Melt the black candy. Stick a heart sprinkle, pointed side up, on either side of each small ball to form the ears. Dip the back of each ball into the black candy and attach it to each white-coated cake ball. One by one, hold each pop by its toothpick and carefully dip the "head" into the black candy, making sure the ears are coated too. Shake off any excess, then run the toothpicks through the wire rack and leave to set.

For the legs, use candy to attach 4 candy-dipped M&M's to the bottom of each pop. Melt the cocoa butter. In the palette, tint 1 teaspoonful each with the 2 dusting powders and leave a third white. On each sheep, paint 2 white dots with a smaller black dot in the middle for the eyes. Use pink to paint the noses.

Remove the toothpicks, place the sheep on a tray lined with parchment paper and leave in the fridge until the cocoa butter has set.

GIRAFFE POPS

My favorite animal just had to be turned into a cake pop. Giraffes are such attractive creatures—don't forget to give them big eyes with long lashes!

Makes 20 pops

Ingredients
20 medium cake balls, chilled
½ (14-ounce) bag each orange and yellow candy melts
40 Tic Tacs
1 bottle white cocoa butter
1 tube each brown and black edible dusting powder

Equipment
Fine paintbrush
Artist's palette

Roll each cake ball into an oblong shape, making one end slightly narrower than the other.

Melt the 2 colors of candy together. Using a toothpick, dab a little candy on each Tic Tac and attach 2 to the top of each pop to represent the horns. Leave to dry.

Dip the end of each lollipop stick ¾ inch deep into the candy. Insert a stick into the bottom of each pop, pushing it through the center of the wider end. Leave to set. Dip each pop fully into the candy and shake off any excess. Insert into a polystyrene block to dry.

Melt the cocoa butter. In the palette, tint 1 teaspoonful each with the 2 dusting powders and leave 1 teaspoonful white. Paint large dots for the eyes with the white color. Use the black color to paint smaller dots into the eyes and then to paint the eyelashes and nostrils. With the brown color paint irregular patches on the giraffe. Place the pops back in the polystyrene block and leave in the fridge until the cocoa butter has set.

MONKEY POPS

These cheeky monkeys are such fun, and quick and easy to put together.

Makes 20 pops

Ingredients
20 medium cake balls, chilled
1 (14-ounce) bag light brown candy melts
2 ounces caramel-color candy melts (or mix ⅓ brown with ⅔ white)
60 chocolate buttons
1 bottle cocoa butter
1 tube black edible dusting powder

Equipment
Thin paintbrush
Artist's palette

Flatten each cake ball slightly. Melt the light brown candy. Using a toothpick, dab a little candy on 40 of the chocolate buttons and attach 1 button to either side of each cake ball for the monkey's ears.

Dip the end of each lollipop stick ¾ inch deep into the candy and insert a stick through bottom of each cake ball. Leave to set. Dip each pop fully into the candy and shake off any excess. Using the remaining chocolate buttons, attach one to the front of each pop and secure in position. Insert into a polystyrene block to dry.

Melt the caramel candy. Scoop up 1 tablespoonful and carefully dip the chocolate button on the front of each pop into the candy. Next, use the candy to paint the inside of the ears and then to paint a heart shape on the top half of the face. Place in the polystyrene block to dry.

Melt the cocoa butter. In the palette, tint 1 teaspoonful with the dusting powder and leave 1 teaspoonful white. Use the white color to paint the eyes. Finally, use the black color to paint black dots on each eye and to paint the nose and mouth on each pop. Place back in the polystyrene block and leave in the fridge for 10 minutes until the cocoa butter has set.

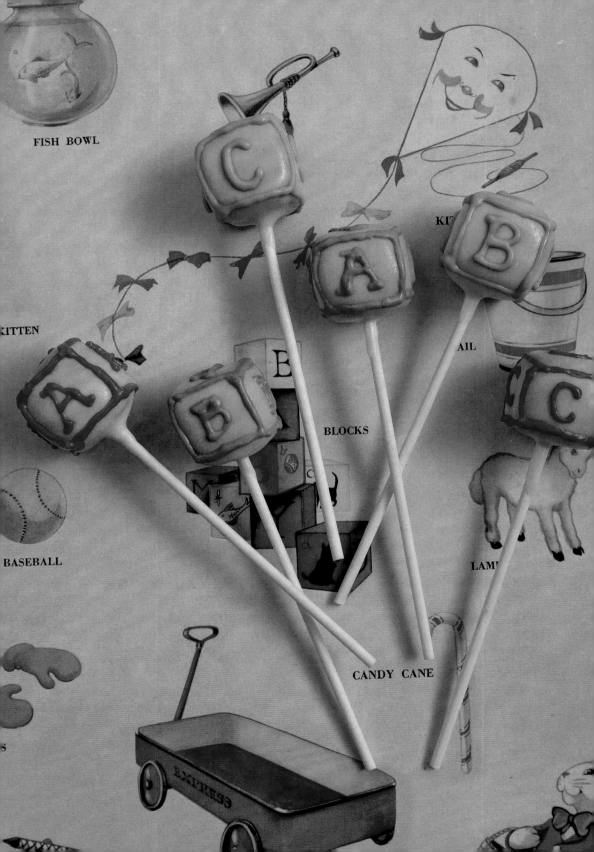

ALPHABET BLOCK POPS

These classic toy pops will transport you right back to childhood. They're perfect for celebrating those early years.

Makes 20 pops

Ingredients
20 cake balls, chilled
1 (14-ounce) bag yellow candy melts
¼ (14-ounce) bag candy melts in blue, green or red

Equipment
Disposable piping bag

Shape each cake ball into a square block, pushing each one against a flat surface to flatten the sides.

Melt the yellow candy. Dip the end of each lollipop stick ¾ inch deep into the candy and insert a stick into each cake ball. Leave to set. Then dip each ball fully into the candy and shake off the excess. Insert into a polystyrene block to dry.

Melt the secondary color of candy, then quickly pour it into the piping bag before the candy sets. Cut a small piece off the tip of the bag. Pipe straight lines of candy all around the edges of the pops. Insert into the polystyrene block to set. Now pipe letters of your choice on each side of the pops. Place back in the polystyrene block to dry.

Tip: if the candy sets before you finish, just place the piping bag in a bowl in the microwave for 10 seconds at a time until it reaches the right consistency.

CLOWN POPS

Surely the most fun you can have with a cake pop? These are bright, colorful and not at all scary. You can choose just one color for the hats or make them in different colors.

Makes 20 pops

Ingredients
20 medium cake balls, chilled
1 (14-ounce) bag white candy melts
2 tablespoons each green, blue and red candy melts
100 grams (just under ½ cup) fondant in different colors of your choice, kneaded
40 grams (2½ tablespoons) red fondant, kneaded
1 bottle colored confetti sprinkles
Edible glue
1 bottle white cocoa butter
1 tube each red and black edible dusting powder

Equipment
2 paintbrushes (1 thin, 1 medium)
Artist's palette

Make in advance
Hats: break the 100 grams (½ cup) fondant into 20 equal pieces and form each one into a hat or cone shape. Using a little edible glue on a paintbrush, secure the confetti sprinkles in place on the shapes. Leave to dry overnight on parchment paper.
Noses: break the red fondant into 20 equal pieces and roll into balls. Leave to dry overnight on parchment paper.

Melt the white candy. Dip the end of each lollipop stick ¾ inch deep into the candy and insert a stick into each cake ball. Leave to set. Now dip each ball fully in the candy and gently tap off the excess. Place a hat on top of each ball while the candy is still wet. Insert into a polystyrene block to dry. Next, attach the noses to the faces as you go, gluing them in place with a dab of candy. Leave to dry.

Melt the additional candy colors separately. Using a toothpick, paint the hair onto each cake pop. Be as creative as you like. The first layer will be very thin, so leave each one to dry before adding another. Gradually build up more layers of hair and use the toothpicks to texturize them. You may need to do this up to 5 times per cake pop. Leave to set.

Next, paint the eyebrows diagonally across the top third of each clown's face, using a dab of candy on a toothpick. Try using contrasting colors for the eyebrows and the hair.

Melt the cocoa butter and tint 1 teaspoonful each with the 2 dusting powders. Paint on a big smiling mouth with the red candy. Paint big black dots for the eyes, then paint lines in the shape of a cross around them. Finally, paint a black line in the middle of the red mouth in the shape of a smile. Place the pops back in the polystyrene block and leave in the fridge for 10 minutes to allow the cocoa butter to set.

Dip the end of each lollipop stick ¾ inch deep into the candy and insert a stick into each snowman. Leave to set. (If the cake balls have softened, place them back in the fridge for 10 minutes.) Dip each pop fully into the white candy and then place a hat on each snowman as you go. Insert into a polystyrene block to dry.

Once the pops have dried, use a toothpick to glue the carrots into the middle of each snowman's face with the remaining white candy.

For the eyes, mouth and buttons: melt the cocoa butter and tint 1 teaspoonful black with the dusting powder. Paint black eyes, mouths and buttons on the snowmen. Insert the pops into the polystyrene block and place in the fridge for about 10 minutes until the cocoa butter has set.

For the scarves, roll out the blue or red fondant, then cut into long, thin strips about 4 inches long and ⅝ inch wide. Working quickly before the fondant dries, attach the scarves to the snowmen by draping them in place. The fondant will glue itself into place as it dries.

CHRISTMAS PUDDINGS

No one will say no to these mini versions of the traditional English Christmas treat. For a really festive touch, make them with Red Velvet Cake or Chocolate Cake (see recipes on pages 26 and 25).

Makes 20 puddings

Ingredients
20 cake balls, chilled
1 (14-ounce) bag dark brown candy melts
¼ (14-ounce) bag white candy melts
Small holly icing decorations

Place a sheet of parchment paper under a wire rack.

Melt the dark brown candy. Insert a toothpick into each cake ball. Dip each fully into the candy, gently shake off any excess and run the toothpicks through the wire rack to dry as you go.

Melt the white candy, adding an extra drop of vegetable oil to make it extra-runny. Using a teaspoon, spoon the candy over the top of each cake and give it a little shake. The candy should start dripping down the sides—if you'd like it to drip more, hold the cake by its toothpick and tap it vertically on a flat surface a couple of times.

While the white candy is still wet, decorate the cakes with the holly icing, then remove the toothpicks and place on a tray lined with parchment paper to dry.

HORROR SHOW POPS

ZOMBIE HEAD POPS

I originally made these for the opening of Eat Your Heart Out, the world's first over-18 cake shop in Shoreditch, East London, where there were hour-long lines for gory cakes. This zombie head design is one of the most fun pops to make.

Makes 20 pops

Ingredients
20 medium cake balls, chilled
1 (14-ounce) bag spooky green candy melts
2 tablespoons pink candy melts
2 ounces red candy melts
40 grams (2½ tablespoons) white fondant, kneaded
1 black and 1 green edible ink pen

Equipment
Disposable piping bag

Make eyes in advance: roll the fondant into 40 small balls. Leave to harden overnight.

Paint the eyes on the fondant, using the black pen for the pupil and the green pen for the iris.
   Shape the cake balls into irregular ovals for the zombie heads. Melt the green candy. Dip the end of each lollipop stick ¾ inch deep in the candy and insert a stick into each cake ball. Leave to set. Dip each cake ball fully into the green candy and shake off the excess. While the candy is still wet, attach an eye on the left side of each face. Insert into a polystyrene block to dry.
   Using a toothpick, dab the green candy around the left eye on each head.
   For the brain, melt the pink candy, then dip the very top of each head into the pink candy and leave to set.
   For the blood, melt the red candy, quickly pour into a piping bag and cut a

small piece off the tip of the bag. For each pop, pipe the eye socket for the right eye in red and place the remaining eyeball over it. Pipe a trail of blood coming out of the eye with the red candy. Now pipe red blood around the pink brain and then pipe drips of blood pouring down the face. Pipe red candy around the stick, then turn the cake pop upside down and give it a little shake. Insert into the polystyrene block to dry.

Using a toothpick, score the pattern of the brain on the top of each pop. Using your finger, dab a little red candy over it and blend it in. Place back in the polystyrene block and leave to set.

EYEBALL POPS

These eyeballs, complete with stalks, look so real. You'd be surprised how many people love to eat cake that looks like body parts. For extra gore make the cake balls with the Red Velvet Cake (see recipe on pages 26 and 22).

Makes 20 pops

Ingredients
20 medium cake balls, chilled
1 (14-ounce) bag white candy melts
2 tablespoons red candy melts
1 bottle white cocoa butter
1 tube each black, green and
  red edible dusting powder

Equipment
Disposable piping bag
2 paintbrushes (1 thin,
  1 medium)
Artist's palette

Melt the white candy. Dip the end of each lollipop stick ¾ inch in the candy and insert a stick into each cake ball. Leave to set. Dip each cake ball fully into the candy and shake off the excess. Insert into a polystyrene block to dry.

Melt the red candy, pour into the piping bag and cut a small piece off the tip of the bag. Pipe the candy over the bottom of the cake pop around the stick to form the root of the eyeball. Leave to set.

Melt the cocoa butter and tint 1 teaspoonful each with the 3 dusting powders. Paint the top of each cake pop with the black color to represent the pupil of the eyeball. Paint the iris around the pupil in green. Then paint red blood vessels around the eyes. Place in the polystyrene block and refrigerate for 10 minutes until the cocoa butter has set.

TECHNIQUES

Over the last 18 months, through trial and quite a bit of error I perfected the art of making cake pops. Looking back I can't believe how much I have learned.

In this section you will find all the tips and tricks you need to get the best results when making cake pops. Learn how to store the individual ingredients at any stage of the popping process, how to paint beautiful designs with cocoa butter and how to make the cutest fondant decorations.

BASIC STORAGE INSTRUCTIONS

You can bake the cake sponge up to three days in advance of making cake pops. It's actually easier to mix the frosting with a cake that's not freshly baked the same day because the crumbs can sometimes be too soft.

If you're able to plan in advance, bake the cake sponge and let it cool. When cool, cover with plastic wrap and store in an airtight container, but don't refrigerate.

You can make the frosting two days in advance but make sure you keep it in the fridge until it's needed. It's best to take it out and leave it at room temperature about two hours before using.

Once you've combined the cake crumbs and frosting, wrap the mixture in plastic wrap and refrigerate. At this point you will need to keep it in the fridge for at least one hour before rolling the cake balls or shapes. If necessary, the cake pop mixture can be kept in the fridge for three days, as can rolled cake balls. Just keep them covered or in an airtight container.

The cake pop mixture and undipped balls can also be frozen for up to three months.

Once dipped, the cake pops can be refrigerated in a plastic airtight container for up to one week.

CAKE BALL SIZES

It's best to make standard sizes of cake balls so they all look the same since this makes it easier to decorate them.

You could weigh each ball on digital scales. A good weight is 30 grams (5 tablespoons). Or you could use a spoon to scoop the mixture and measure the size you want. As a guide, 1 tablespoon of cake pop mixture makes a small cake ball about 1¼ inch in diameter, and 2 tablespoons makes a medium-sized, 1½-inch-diameter ball.

SHAPING CAKE BALLS

If you combine it properly, the mixture for cake pops is very versatile. You can

mold it into all sorts of different shapes without it falling apart. This is great when it comes to making more elaborate designs. You can roll into long strips or taper it into cone shapes.

The ball tool is commonly used in cake decorating. I like to use it for detailing, such as the perfectly rounded indentations in the Donut Pops and the eyes in the Skull Pops. But if you don't have a ball tool, you can use your index finger just as well.

GLUING

For big gluing jobs, such as sticking two bits of cake ball together, it is best to use candy melts. You don't want your pops to fall apart and candy melts are surprisingly stubborn when they have dried. They will hold anything together!

For more detailed gluing work like sticking on fondant decorations, use edible glue. With a paintbrush and edible glue you get a much finer finish so it is perfect for adding the finishing touches to designs that have already been painted.

OTHER USEFUL TOOLS FOR DECORATING

Paintbrushes: for painting pretty designs onto cake pops with cocoa butter or for piecing fondant decorations together with edible glue.

Artist's palette: for mixing and coloring cocoa butter.

CREATING DIFFERENT COLORS WITH CANDY MELTS

You can mix different colors of candy melts together to create new ones. If you need to lighten the color, just add some white candy melts. Alternatively, you can use oil-based candy colors to tint white candy melts. To color candy this way, start with a tiny drop of oil-based color and stir. Keep adding a drop at a time until you reach the desired shade.

Note: Like chocolate, candy is oil-based, so do not mix it with water and don't use normal, non-oil-based food colorings with candy melts.

TIPS FOR MANAGING CANDY MELTS

Working out how much candy to use per project is tricky as it depends on your dipping skills, the size of the cake pops and what consistency you want to achieve. For a beginner, I would say that you will need a whole bag (14 ounces) for 20 cake pops, half a bag (7 ounces) for 10 cake pops, a quarter bag (3½ ounces) for 5 pops, and so on. Use this as a guide to work out how much candy to use when you want to mix different colors in each batch.

Most instructions say you can't reheat candy, but I have successfully re-melted it. Just add a drop of vegetable oil before putting it into the microwave. When piping candy onto cake pops, should you find the candy sets before you finish, just place the piping bag in a bowl in the microwave for 10 seconds at a time until it reaches the right consistency.

If you have lots of candy left over after making cake pops, it's always worth trying to save it. Using a spatula, spread it over a sheet of parchment paper and leave to set. Once it has set, break it up and store in a plastic food bag at room temperature.

MAKING FONDANT DECORATIONS

Fondant is the rolled icing often used to cover cakes. In this book it is used to make beautiful decorations to add to cake pops. Good-quality fondant is widely available from cake craft shops or online (see page 146 for suppliers).

You can make a whole variety of fondant decorations to apply to cake pops by using tools such as pastry cutters and silicone molds. I have given instructions in the individual recipes for making the specific decorations for each cake pop design in this book, but use the directions below as a guide to preparing fondant and to making decorations using silicone molds.

Before you start to work with fondant you must knead it to make it pliable. First you will need to add a powder called gum tragacanth—1 teaspoon per 500 grams (2 cups) is required. This makes the fondant strong and elastic. Using your hands, knead the powder into the fondant to warm it up. Keep kneading for about 5 minutes until the fondant stretches like chewing gum when you pull it apart.

To color fondant, simply dab a little food coloring (normal food coloring paste is fine) on the fondant with a toothpick and knead until the color is consistent and not streaky. Repeat until your desired shade is achieved.

You can stick individual parts of the fondant decorations together with some edible glue applied with a paintbrush. To attach fondant decorations to cake pops, use a dab of candy melt on a toothpick.

Fondant can dry out easily so, when not in use, store in an airtight container. If you find it has dried out slightly, you can apply a little vegetable shortening such as Crisco to fondant before using.

MAKING FONDANT DECORATIONS BY HAND

You'll want to make some fondant designs for which there isn't a mold. The good news is fondant is very easy to work with. It's like modeling clay so you can shape it by hand before painting and decorating it. So long as you knead it, it will be pliable and stretchy. You can flatten it into disks, squish it into beads and roll it into tubes. It'll shape itself into anything from teapot lids and handles to a snowman's scarf and earmuffs!

Make sure your hands are clean and free from water when handling fondant, and it's best to wear light clothing too as fondant has a tendency to pick up stray fibers.

If you plan to make sugar decorations often, it's useful to invest in a nonstick board to work on.

USING FONDANT WITH SILICONE MOLDS

Silicone molds enable you to make a wide variety of different decorations to add character to cake pops. You can buy a huge range of molds online (see page 146 for suppliers). With diverse themes such as flowers, balloons, faces, sports, fashion, as well as seasonal molds, you can find something for every occasion.

Try to judge how much fondant will fit into each mold—you simply push it in, smooth your finger over it and pop it out seconds later. If you find you have used too little, just add more and smooth it out. If you have used too much, then cut off the excess with a knife. Leave to dry on parchment paper.

Fondant decorations should ideally be made in advance so they can dry fully before you use them on cake pops—about 2 days in advance is perfect, but the day before is also fine. They can be stored in plastic airtight containers for several weeks.

For a beautiful shimmer effect, spray them with edible luster or apply a little edible glue with a paintbrush and then sprinkle with edible glitter.

USING COCOA BUTTER FOR PAINTING

The easiest and most effective way to paint designs or patterns on cake pops is by using cocoa butter, which you melt first (see below) and then apply with a paintbrush. You can buy cocoa butter in bottles from specialist chocolate-making suppliers (see page 146 for retailers).

Cocoa butter comes in various colors but, when working with different colors, I like to use white cocoa butter and then tint it with edible dusting powder, which is food coloring in powder form. This is more cost-effective than buying different colors of cocoa butter. It is worth investing in a bottle as a little goes a long way.

To melt the cocoa butter, put the bottle into the microwave. Heat for 1 minute, shake the bottle well, heat for 1 minute more then shake again. Once the cocoa butter has reached liquid consistency, pour 1 teaspoonful into an artist's palette. To color it, sprinkle a little edible dusting powder into the cocoa butter and stir with a paintbrush. It's easy to tint cocoa butter in pastel colors but it can be tricky to get a true black or red. So keep adding a little more powder until you reach the desired shade. Colors can also be mixed together to create new shades. Repeat with as many colors as needed.

Any unused cocoa butter can be stored in the bottle at room temperature and the butter can be re-melted as many times as you like.

Cocoa butter is very fluid and easy to work with but has a tendency to dry out very quickly. The good news is that you can keep returning the artist's palette to the microwave for 10-second bursts. When you have finished painting, you can cover any leftover cocoa butter in the palette with plastic wrap and reuse when needed. There's no need to refrigerate it.

Once you have painted the cake pops, you will need to put them on a tray lined with parchment paper and place them in the fridge for 10–15 minutes to allow the cocoa butter to set, otherwise your beautiful work will smudge.

USING EDIBLE INK PENS

These are excellent for drawing designs and patterns on fondant. You can also use them instead of cocoa butter for drawing on cake pops, although they are not as fluid and tend to dry out quickly.

The pens come in a variety of colors and the best brand is Americolor (see page 146 for suppliers).

PACKAGING AND PRESENTATION

Cake pops look even more beautiful when wrapped in little plastic bags. Just slip them into the bag and seal with a twist tie or a pretty ribbon.

They also make attractive gifts when presented in a chocolate box or small cake box. Line the box with colored tissue paper first.

If you're making cake pops for a party and want to display them, try wrapping some polystyrene in printed paper or tissue paper and stick the pops in it. You could even make a tiered display with different-sized cake dummies. Vases filled with sprinkles also work well. Use the pages in this book as inspiration.

SUPPLIERS

Cake pops and supplies such as lollipop sticks, twist ties, display stands
and handmade decorations
www.mollybakes.co.uk

Cake decorating equipment and twist ties
www.cakesupply.com
www.kitchencrafts.com

Cake making ingredients are available from most major supermarkets and many
online retailers.
www.wholefoodsmarket.com (organic flour, unrefined sugar)
www.equalexchange.coop (fairtrade organic cocoa powder)

Candy coloring, candy melts, edible ink pens, edible glitter and fondant
equipment
www.michaels.com
www.wilton.com

Cocoa butter and edible dusting powder
www.candylandcrafts.com

Edible sprinkles, rose and violet petals, candy coloring oils and flavors
www.thebakerskitchen.net

Silicone molds, including rose molds and vintage button molds
www.firstimpressionmolds.com

INDEX

ACKNOWLEDGMENTS

Thanks to my mum who taught me how to bake, my dad for encouraging me to start selling my cakes, my sisters for all the hours of free help, and to my fiancé Olly for putting up with all the baking madness and putting the Olly into Molly.

To Rowan for giving me this fantastic opportunity and the rest of the wonderful team who have made this book so beautiful: Fred, Noel and Wei. Special thanks to my two assistants Heather and Chloe. Thanks also to Cristian and Joe for their support.

Last but not least, thanks to Miss Cakehead for all the genius cake events she has organized, which inspired some of the edgier designs in this book.

OTHER ULYSSES PRESS BOOKS

Grace's Sweet Life: Homemade Italian Desserts from Cannoli, Biscotti, and Tiramisu to Torte, Tartufi, and Struffoli
Grace Massa-Langlois, $14.95
Author Grace Massa-Langlois shows you how to make classic homemade Italian treats just like Grandma. From espresso-rich tiramisu, cannoli overflowing with ricotta or rich and creamy tartufo, *Grace's Sweet Life* presents the 75 most popular, reader-tested recipes from the author's popular website.

The I Love Trader Joe's Cookbook: Over 150 Delicious Recipes Using Only Foods from the World's Greatest Grocery Store
Cherie Mercer Twohy, $17.95
Based on the author's wildly popular, standing-room-only workshops, *The I Love Trader Joe's Cookbook* presents her top recipes for everything from crowd-pleasing hors d'oeuvres and tasty quick meals to gourmet entrées and world-class desserts.

The I Love Trader Joe's Party Cookbook: Delicious Recipes and Entertaining Ideas Using Only Foods and Drinks from the World's Greatest Grocery Store
Cherie Mercer Twohy, $17.95
With menus and plans for more than 25 celebrations, this indispensable entertaining guide is packed with mouthwatering recipes, do-ahead tips, and drink suggestions.

Macarons: Authentic French Cookie Recipes from the Macaron Café
Cecile Cannone, $14.95
Cuter than a cupcake and more delicious, the adorable macaron is *très en vogue*. Now you can make these crowd-pleasing cookies at home! Packed with helpful and inspiring color photos, this book offers everything you need to bake stunning macarons.

Mini Pies: Adorably Delicious Recipes for Your Favorite Treats

Christy Beaver and Morgan Greenseth, $14.95

With enticing color photographs, this book shows you how to use a cupcake pan to bake the newest, most awesome dessert—mini pies. Offering step-by-step recipes along with tips, tricks and techniques for mini pie success, this book teaches you how to make flaky crusts and luscious fillings that will combine into mouthwatering petite pies.

Sugar-Free Gluten-Free Baking and Desserts: Recipes for Healthy and Delicious Cookies, Cakes, Muffins, Scones, Pies, Puddings, Breads and Pizzas

Kelly Keough, $14.95

Shows readers how to bring taboo treats back to the baking sheet with savory recipes that swap wheat for wholesome alternatives like quinoa, arrowroot and tapioca starch, and trade in sugar for natural sweeteners like agave, yacon and stevia.

Who You Callin' Cupcake?: 75 In-Your-Face Recipes That Reinvent the Cupcake

Michelle Garcia & Vinny Garcia, $15.95

You don't need to be a master chef to use this book's easy-to-follow system for making cupcakes as daring as they are delicious, like Bananas Foster, Creamsicle, Curry Cardamom, White Chocolate Wasabi, and even BBQ Pork.

To order these books call 800-377-2542 or 510-601-8301, fax 510-601-8307, e-mail ulysses@ulyssespress.com, or write to Ulysses Press, P.O. Box 3440, Berkeley, CA 94703. All retail orders are shipped free of charge. California residents must include sales tax. Allow two to three weeks for delivery.

"Molly Bakes," as she is known when baking, is surprisingly new to cakes. Two years ago, on the eve of her birthday, she found herself out of a job. Rather than mope, she took up baking for the very first time. She fell in love and has never looked back. Today her cake pops can be found everywhere from her stall at Brick Lane Market to Selfridges department store, and include clients such as *Vogue* and fans like Eliza Doolittle.